MY CONSCIOUSNESS

KILL YOUR DARKNESS

ISHIKA VERMA

This book is dedicated to all the people out there who overcame all thier fears. You are a true warrior.

Contents

Contents

Preface

This book has short poetries having deep thoughts and inner consciousness. These poetries has different angles with same observations. There are many peole living out there questioning themselves. These poetries will give words to your feelings. It will make you feel empowered.

1. who knows

we dont look at each other with the same perspective,

those perspectives are somewhere restrictive.

you find love in me and i find hope in you,

now we both see our sky same as blue.

i was like a child lost in between crying for help,

you was like an angel in heaven, my lucky whelp.

i was like a sea never meeting the end of the shore,

you was like a wind who reach anywhere with flow.

you and me together are a perfect fit like Cinderella's shoes,

but these all are my imaginations and here who knows who?

2. blockbuster or disaster

beautiful faces will be dead one day, but beautiful souls will live everyday.

your smell will attract many, but your behavior will distract many.

some are called gold diggers, and some are hole diggers.

some surrender their hearts for real, but they are the one who live in fear.

the system of this entire love is hard, some find it at end and some at start.

but how can we say they are the one for us, we ourselves are not even trying, plus.

i dont think anything like perfect exist, imperfects together make it resist.

how can we take next step at all? when our previous step is still at role?

why me? isn't the appropriate question, only what matters is others actions.

it can either be a blockbuster, or it can only create disaster.

3. ability to forget

• 3 •

nobody matches to my taste now days,

as my tastebuds are dead in every ways.

sometimes i just wanna love someone so bad,

but sometimes i just want to shout loud.

i am feeling like a slime, shaping myself with rhyme.

i just can't get over the undone past, but i want to get it over just like a roast.

i am in no mood to lie down and cry everyday. i just want a place where i can stay just stay.

i am a person living in an online world but basically i want love letters on hold.

maybe i want to quit the idea of reliability, because i am loosing my every ability.

ability to trust, ability to respect, for once i just want to forget.

4. a faith that does not fade

• 4 •

these little smiles can never be enough,
because to smile with whole heart is tough.
slowly the entire manuscript will retire,
because these will not suit our attire.
it might take years for the sea to reach the shore,
but when life if taking a break it might need more.
reading things in one go will not lead to the conclusions.
these mind games will only and only create confusions.
be the person who have their own faith in them,
because we know every thing here is just condemn.

5. a pure thought

what should we feel when we dont feel at all?
here in this dramatic play what's my role?
thoughts needs to be pure and gigantic?
but why can't it always become romantic?
sometimes harsh reality feels so satisfying,
that i feel okay without even rectifying.
i need some real values to depend upon,
sometimes its perfect to become like stone.
my ankles twist everytime, every second i try to fly,
obviously i dont have real wings but still i try.
because without trying how will i know my worth,
to learn, to live, to be happy is my right by birth.

6. should i stop?

i am still in a blanket all day resting like nothing, like nothing is left to do that i have everything.

but the reality is far far away and bitter than i think, or atleast what i assume with a thought that shrink.

creases all over clothes feels like snakes, to achieve the relief what will it take?

feels like i am just a pin with no importance, but pin can also stich the entire wardrobe sense.

so should i be proud of me laying in silence? or should i shout and shout and create violence?

the more time i want to have to make a decision, the more i am nervous and again doing revision.

some feelings can't be washed just by rinsing, i am lying alone while my phone is still ringing.

the ability to respond to make efforts is dying, is that what i want? or what it is that i am applying?

7. great show

maybe you are not the one whom i will chase,
because even your presence doesn't create craze.
i might be feeling low under my pillow,
but you are the one whom i can't follow.
your smell your touch no longer effects my brain,
that's the reason i am here without getting insane.
the darkness you spill on my thoughts is limitless,
even my own spirit can't be stop with a harness.
i admired me in a way that i found me at a point,
that somehow i am alive and can't get disappoint.
may your soul be brave enough to let me go,
trust me with me you put up a great show.

8. if i was you

if i was you then maybe life would be different,
different in every aspect with a clear concept.
i can walk miles barefoot just to see you smile,
because i am like that only its my idea my style.
who knows if you were me what would happen?
because you could not be able to handle.
Handle all the trauma caused,
how can it be disposed?
life would be paused for a moment,
but will that moment be relevant?

9. my god knows

i know my god knows who i am, for that i don't need your stamp.

believe it or not you are under observation, observed by that supreme power of all nations.

if you think you can rest in peace when you die, just remember you have to answers all the why.

thats why did you heart those innocent hearts, the one which is very pure by every stories start.

oh my dear it's true that karma is a real bad bitch, who doesn't favour anybody, no poor, no rich.

you think your bad deeds can be forgiven? because even the things get away when striven.

the pain felt all over and inside should be left aside, beleive it and let the god sitting over sky decide.

let set the sorrows on fire, wishing for our desire, let your pain sink and take your peace higher.

10. fault on my part

years passed but i am still having your thoughts,
sipping my tea having romantic scenarios.
but eventually i stopped living in the past,
because its not love when it can't last.
i was not assuming nor i was thinking,
it was you who made me do the overthinking.
millions of reasons were there,
then also i look for answers everywhere.
good things come to good hearts,
was my heart not good? that you tore it apart.
mere allegations can't be enough i know,
but with you it was entirely the scripted show.
i believed that you will never decieve.
there was a fault on my part that i believe,

11. we are a miracle

• 11 •

No i am not gonna promise you star and moon, because trust me
people say and forget this soon.
i will be lying next to you till your last breath, i will be there, be only
yours until i face death.
no matter what destiny plan for you and me, we are still us, in my eyes
you can always see.
as my words will not be flattering enough, because my eyes will not be
doing any bluff.
all i want to say is already you have felt, let the love beneath your chest
melt.
let these eyes collide, let my heart decide.
i am here you just have to feel, together we both gonna deal.
deal with every obstacles, oh baby we are a miracle

12. what we got

At first i thought you were my dream come true, but it was never ever our dream it was just you.

you were making your own rash decisions, killing inside me was just my imaginations.

i hope someday you realise that i am just me, nonone literally noone can be me if you see.

nobody could know in advance what you want, nobody could ever be enough, does it haunt?

i thought you and i are just one thing, the thing for me which meant everything.

but suddenly, that thing collapsed, and the reason can never be passed.

you know why? because it was you, you killed my hope to have a better view.

it doesn't matter what you want what i want, what matters is what we want, and what we got.

just ask your heart once was it anyhow fair? that you are laughing there and i am dead here.

13. i live before i die

i may be too expressive and you may be not, but its because we are here to balance the both.

something's i will express on your behalf, baby its love and i wannabe your better half.

from waking up in the morning together, to sleep in each others arms forever.

am i expecting too much? i just wanna feel your touch.

its true that you complete me, so why do you cheated on me?

was it because i loved you more? and if not then what was it for?

you may think that i am very forgiving, but dear i am not any machine of love making.

if i have to choose now between you and me, it will always be me because i want to get free.

Free from your thoughts and lies, so that i live, i live before i die.

14. for better life

yes i am hiding my emotions under the pillow, if i tell you so will you chase them and follow?
because seems like for me it was always be you, no matter where i go no matter what i do its you,
but i didn't saw, that for you it was never me, its never me or me it was just you see.
i am noone to complaint because i am nothing, it took me years to understand what's coming.
i can't live my entire life behind one moment, and even that moment was not so permanant.
i assure you that i loved you million times, but together from you i don't get that signs.
once you was a most special part of my heart, but my destiny says that i have to erase the past.
for the better life with peace in my arms, i have to remove your memory and your charms.

15. stay

just stay with me little more its just afternoon, lie down under the stars with me to stare moon.

cut the crap and lets hold each other for life, just before you die live with me and feel alive.

attachments can be made anywhere, but detachments hits everywhere.

no days, no months, no years can be counted, "don't leave by giving scars" my soul shouted.

inch by inch my heart stopped feeling of relief, i lied there with my pain on the floor, just believe.

i am unable to open that scar that took me so far, far from your love just like a diminishing star.

i can't hate you because just like heart needs air, like that only my life needs you to be right here.

they say you are drowning in his love forsure, but I say even if i forget then also there is no cure.

16. make your tomorrow

your today's will be your power for tomorrow, believe in self power, and don't let it borrow.

because investing in some things will only make you proud, be the person who wants to achieve, don't just roam around.

if you will give time to yourself today, people will be waiting for your time tomorrow.

build your today with a better way, don't just stay there, please don't stay.

all the problems will be blocmed like a flower, you just need some patience like a superpower.

I believe that beautiful things are made on sacrifices, its not compulsory its only upon your choices.

make a life that will be remembered by many, because people today will only take your penny.

Chapter17

I was walking along the path while i am still freeze,
because i Don't understand how to act and choose.
if i choose the right one then is it meant for me?
and even if i Choose the left one do i get free?
i am still wondering that somehow i run away,
but my mind says its alright just stay just stay.
the burden of thinking is too much to bear,
and at one point I just want to share and share.
the things can be beautiful someday,
flowers will bloom on a sunny day.
the surroundings will give you all the support, j
ust waiting and waiting to get escort.

18. the one

my dark thoughts takes me to the dark world, yes its true what you just heard.

my paths are diminishing even in lights, what else i can do except giving it a fight.

noone actually cares, even when we share.

those are lucky enough who got a hand to hold, even though life is still cold.

my life needs no shining star, because i have come so far.

all i ever wanted was destiny to be fulfilled, which makes life happy and thrilled.

go away, go away they said, but all they want was someone to understand.

give it a chance for the one you care for, make some efforts from your every core.

19. my heart needs answers

sometimes i wish i could run to the land where no one exist,
because my heart needs an exit.
exit from all the chaos and chase
its my emotions, not any phrase
i die, i die each and every moment
because nothing holds me permanent
i want to stick to all the peace
but its breaking me piece by piece
i am feeling like an fool, crying from inside
my heart needs all the answers, it has to decide

20. blame game

today's generation does not know how to make efforts, they only know how to see flaws and defects.

you may call me the old school one, but oh dear problems i never run.

i can run miles and miles just to see that smile, maybe its my nature who needs to fly with its own aile.

yes life can be changed in a minute, dear, sometimes it makes you live in a total fear.

wish i could be like others, because then it doesn't make me bothered.

no matter how hard i try, it will always going to me who cry.

blaming anyone is not my nature, i blame my destiny and myself as a creature.

for once can i also become cold hearted? because i was the one who is always taken for granted

21. trust shiva

• 21 •

all my trust was shattered away in a minute, then the lord shiva told me that it wasn't permanent.

i asked him is my destiny planned like this? he said "make yourself believe in peace".

then i asked him again does this cycle of pain will ever end?

he said "believe me, just make yourself stand".

no matter how hard things get today, you have a better future waiting tomorrow with a hope of ray".

did i asked something more than what i deserve? he said "you trust upon me, I will never let you down".

the only one in this world in whome i believe is you,

the people who wants to hurt you are standing in a que.

i am not able to trust anybody now, whats the solution?

he said " a ray of hope will come after rain, just come out of your imaginations.

22. my worth

if its meants to be with you,
it will stay, you don't have to force that in any way.
if it belongs to you it will be there,
you don't have to make it repair.
true bonds are never made forcefully,
if the love is actually true, it will stay truely.
if you are worthy enough, you never have to wait,
get charge of your life and make it update.

23. giving up hope

• 23 •

in the middle of that dark night,

somehow we all are giving a fight.

scared of attachments, in the process of detachment.

everytime i open up it hurts, feels like i am lost in some desert.

should we stop believing?

because honey, its killing.

killing from head to toe, what else life will show.

seems like am giving up on hope,

because dear i am unable to cope.

24. i was extra

from Stanger to my priority, it took place,
but seems like i don't have to chase.
because if it stayed, it will bloom,
if left in pain, I will just assume.
back to Stangers again,
surely it will make me insane.
opening and sharing my soul is not easy,
but seems like i am the one feeling dizzy.
that extra efforts, extra time, extra care,
but i was the extra not rare.
footprints are not leaving, heart is still not breathing.
please show me the mercy, i am forgetting the courtesy.

25. stand for yourself

• 25 •

just because you are giving your all doesn't mean the other person will also do the same,

believe it or not, one day they will forget your name.

sometimes I wonder life should be like a traffic signal where wait is worn it,

where you and your expectations get fit.

if somebody is home to you that doesn't mean you are home for them,

if that's true they have treated you like a gem.

stop expecting start accepting. no matter if things doesn't fall in your favour, it doesn't matter if you don't get the same care.

you believe in gods plan waiting for you to reach the end.

make yourself stand and let that god make amend.

26. my heart

I was lying on that soft mattress,
I was seeing the roof top chanting mantras.
That showed me the way to new ray,
But actually my soul was getting played.
Remembering the times when i failed.
I might fight for you to my last end,
But then also you will not understand.
You didn't fight to keep me in your life,
This thing is cutting my heart with a knife.
I know i know that i am not perfect at all,
You kicked me out like i am a football.
will i open my heart's window again?
Because every core and part is broken.
My emotions has wrapped me into sadness,
I want to unlock all the doors of madness.

27. drowning in love

why does my heart still ache for you?
why can't i focus on myself instead of you?
please stop all these noises inside my head,
its drowing me, feels like i am all dead.
breathing but not living, i have stopped believing.
what does all that promises meant,
when it wasn't permanent.
i believed you from the start,
you knew everything still you broke my heart.

28. soul is sinking

why can't you become mean like everyone out there?
you are okay or not, who cares?
my soul doesn't want to sink in this situation.
but how can i overcome these imaginations?
opening up your soul is not at all easy,
when hurted again and again, you go all crazy.

29. moon

• 29 •

even the moon told me that you are better alone,
why do you care about them who are gone.
look at me, i am alone and i still shine,
sweetheart you are beautiful and fine.
the more you think, the more you sink
learn to rise, because you are wise.

30. your choice

whatever happens in your life its meant to make you strong enough,
if life is giving you lessons then just take it and make yourself tough.
there is a new day after every sunrise,
you want to get up or not its your choice.
maybe if you wake up one day,
all the happiness will always stay.